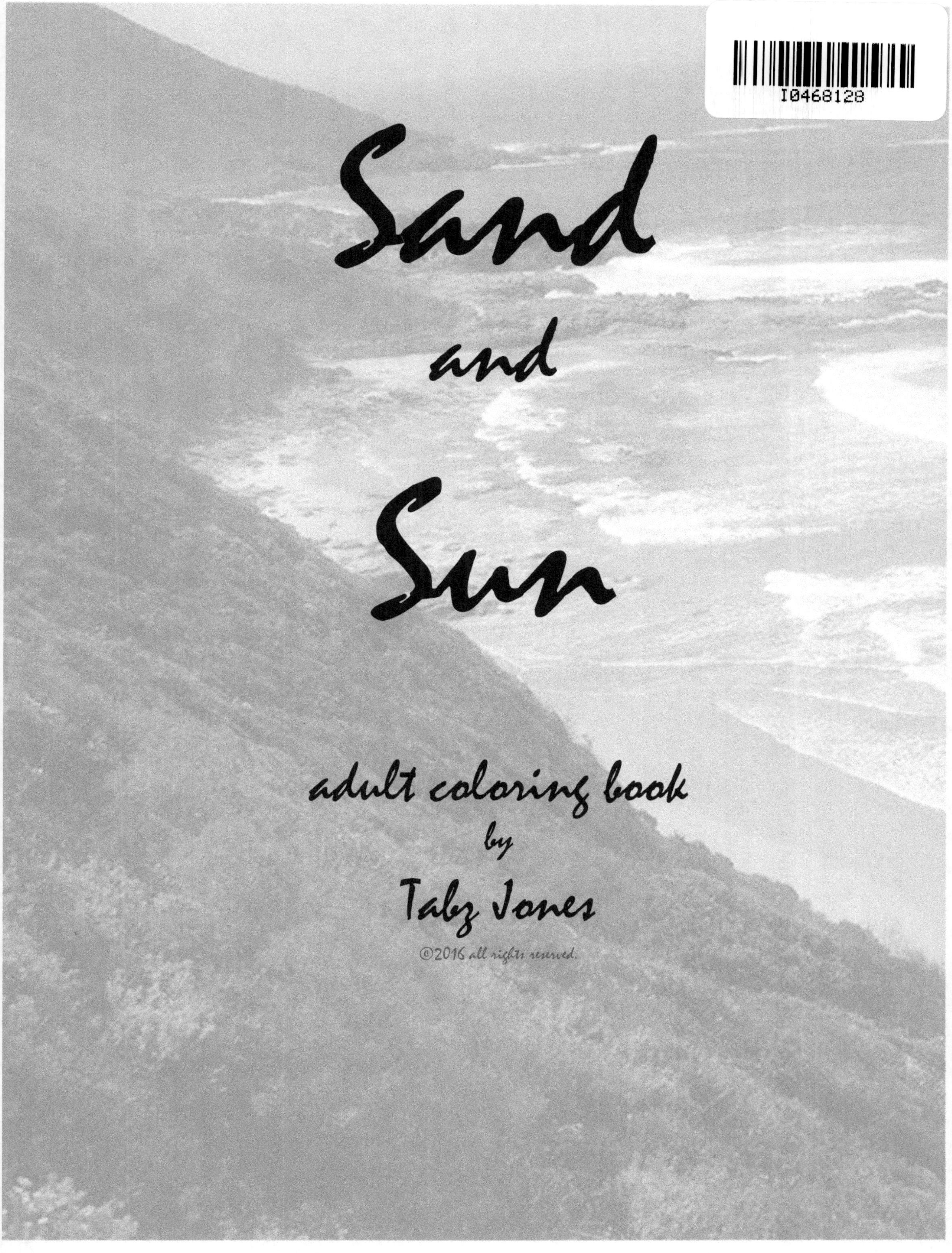

Sand and Sun

adult coloring book

by

Tabz Jones

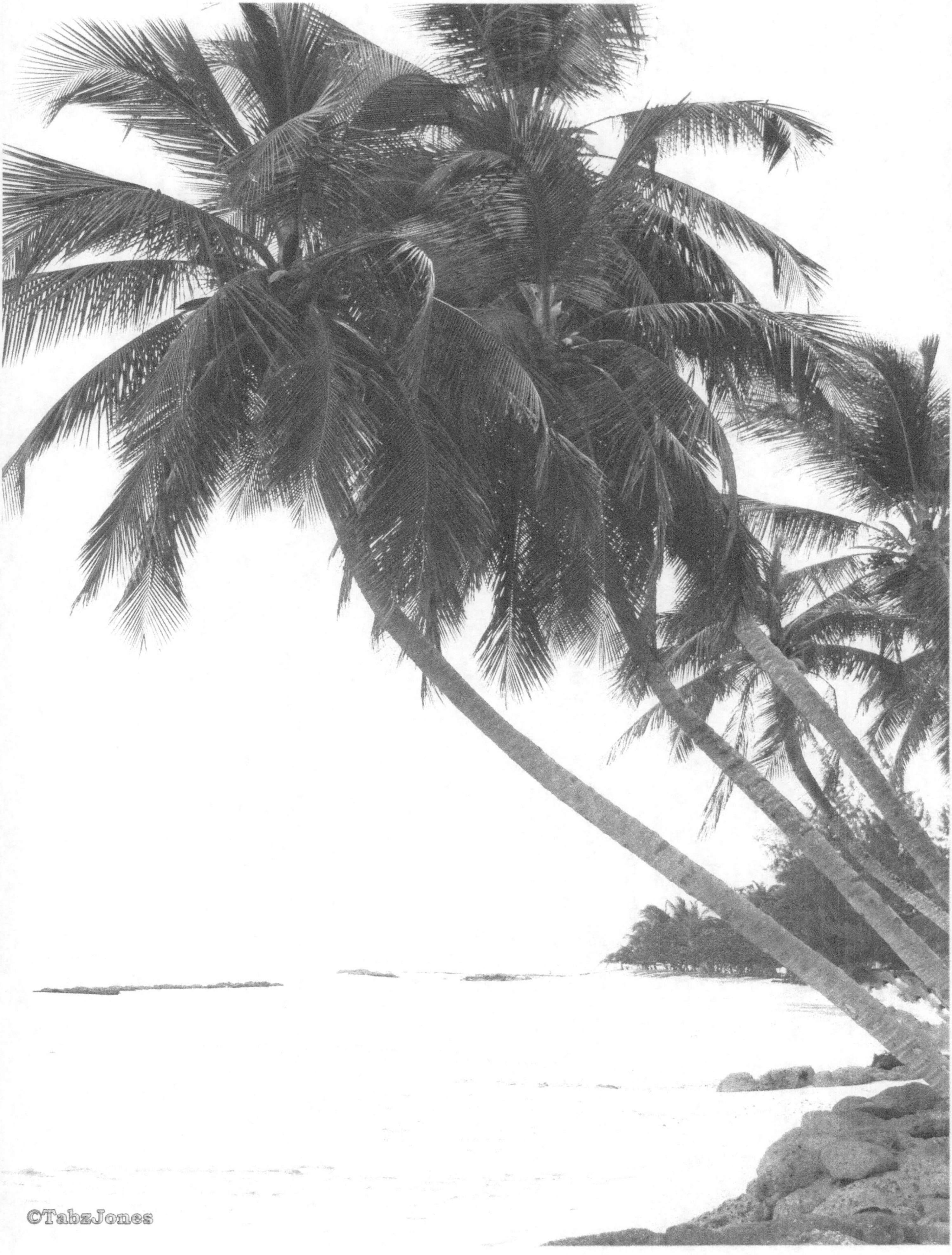

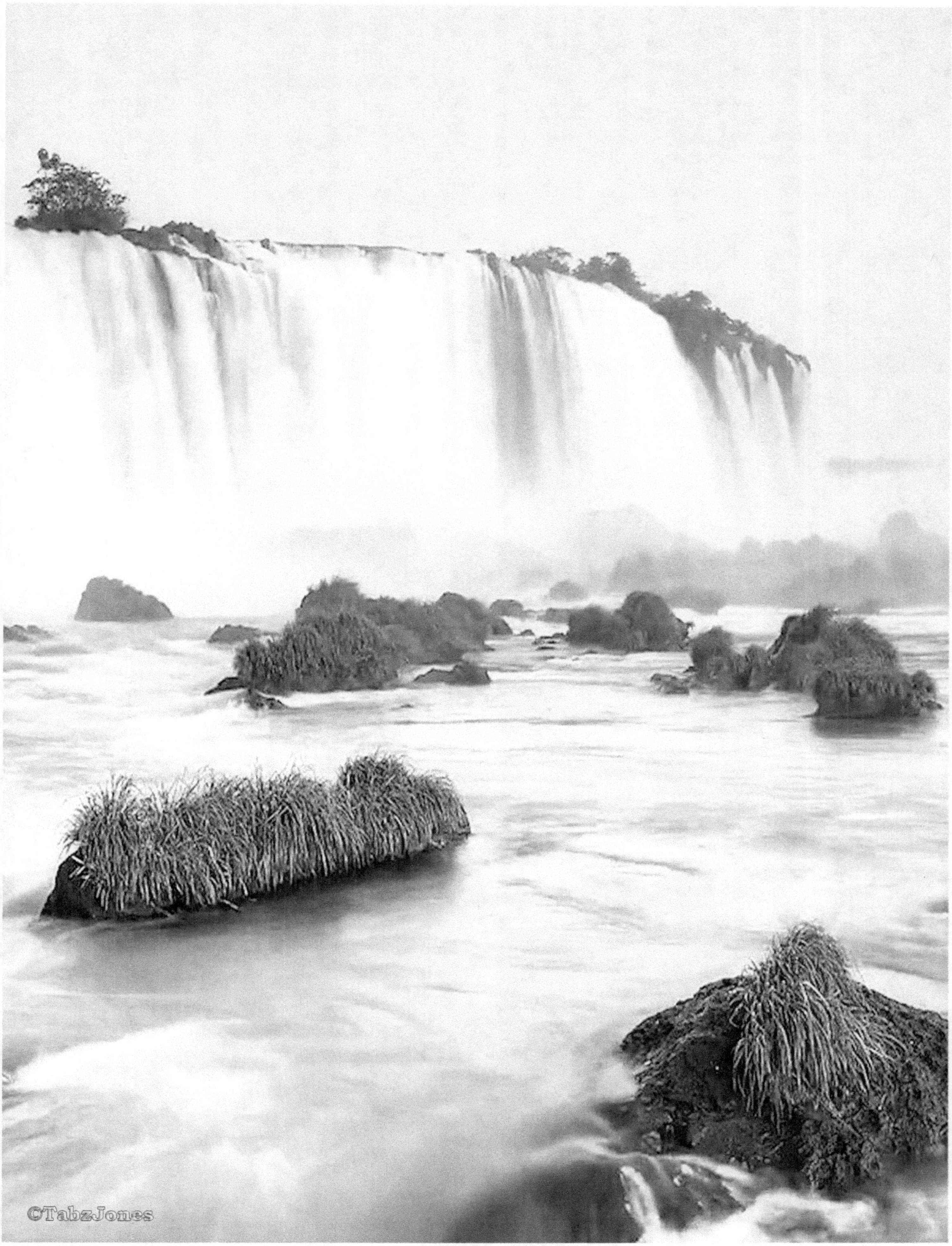
©TabzJones

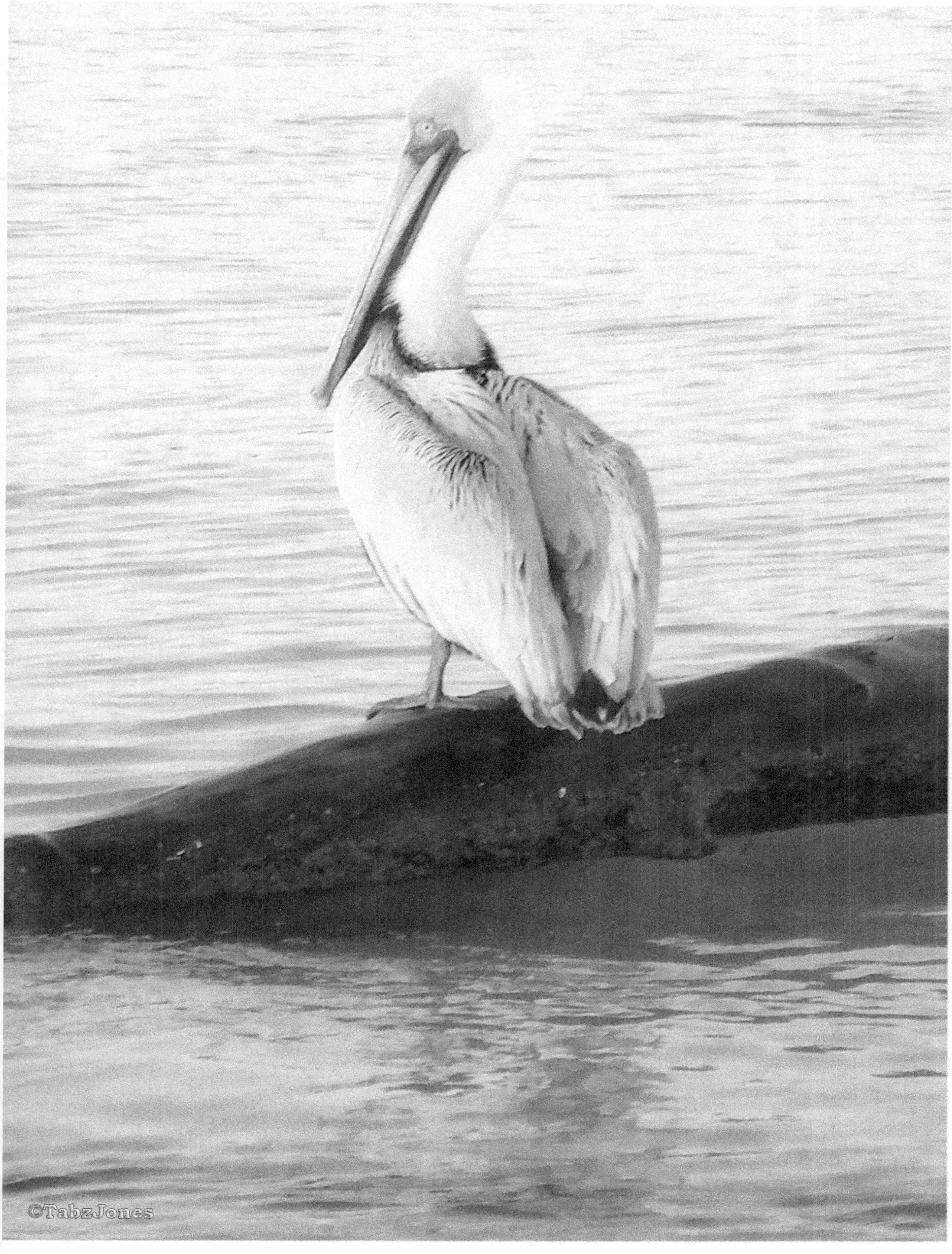
©TabzJones

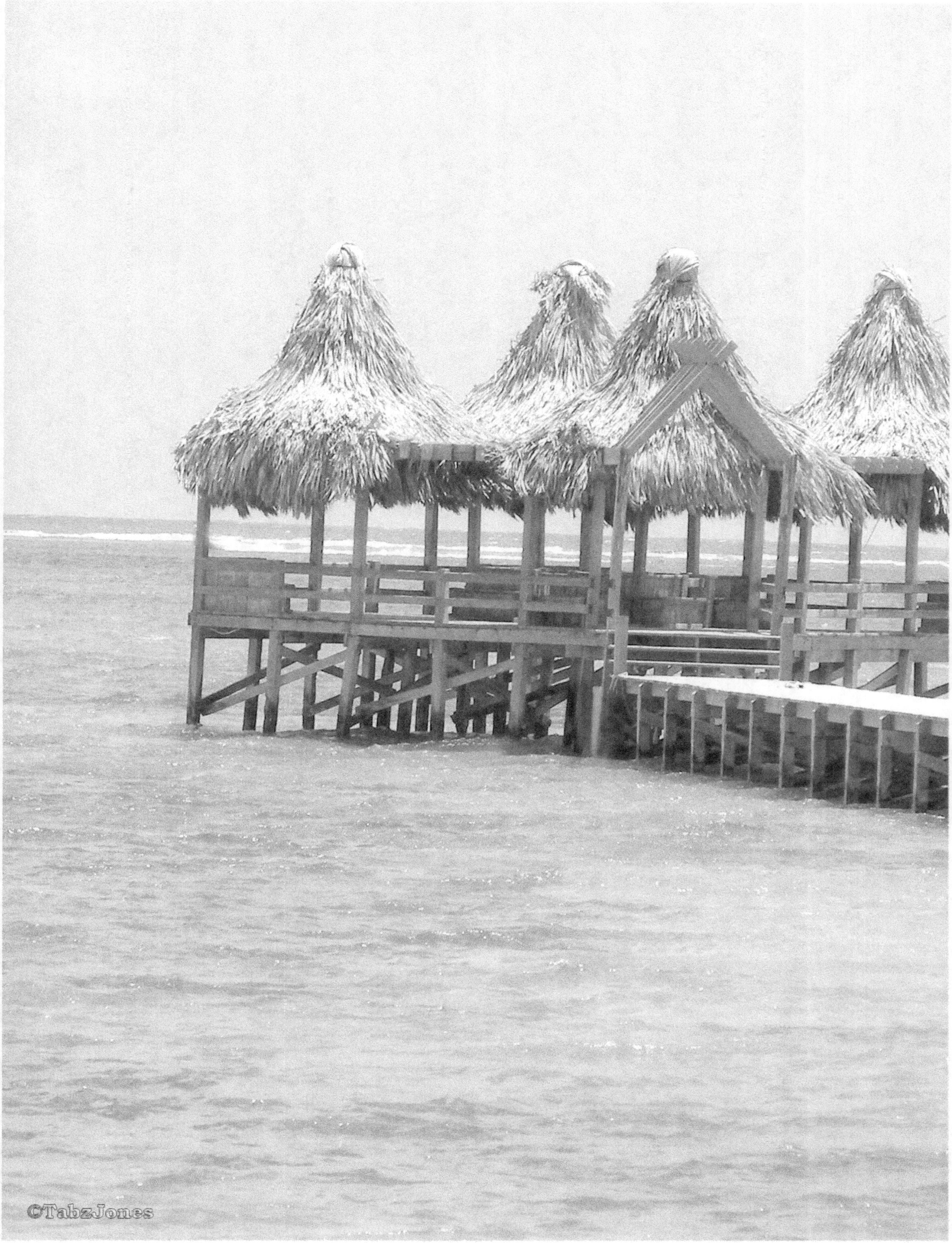
©TabzJones

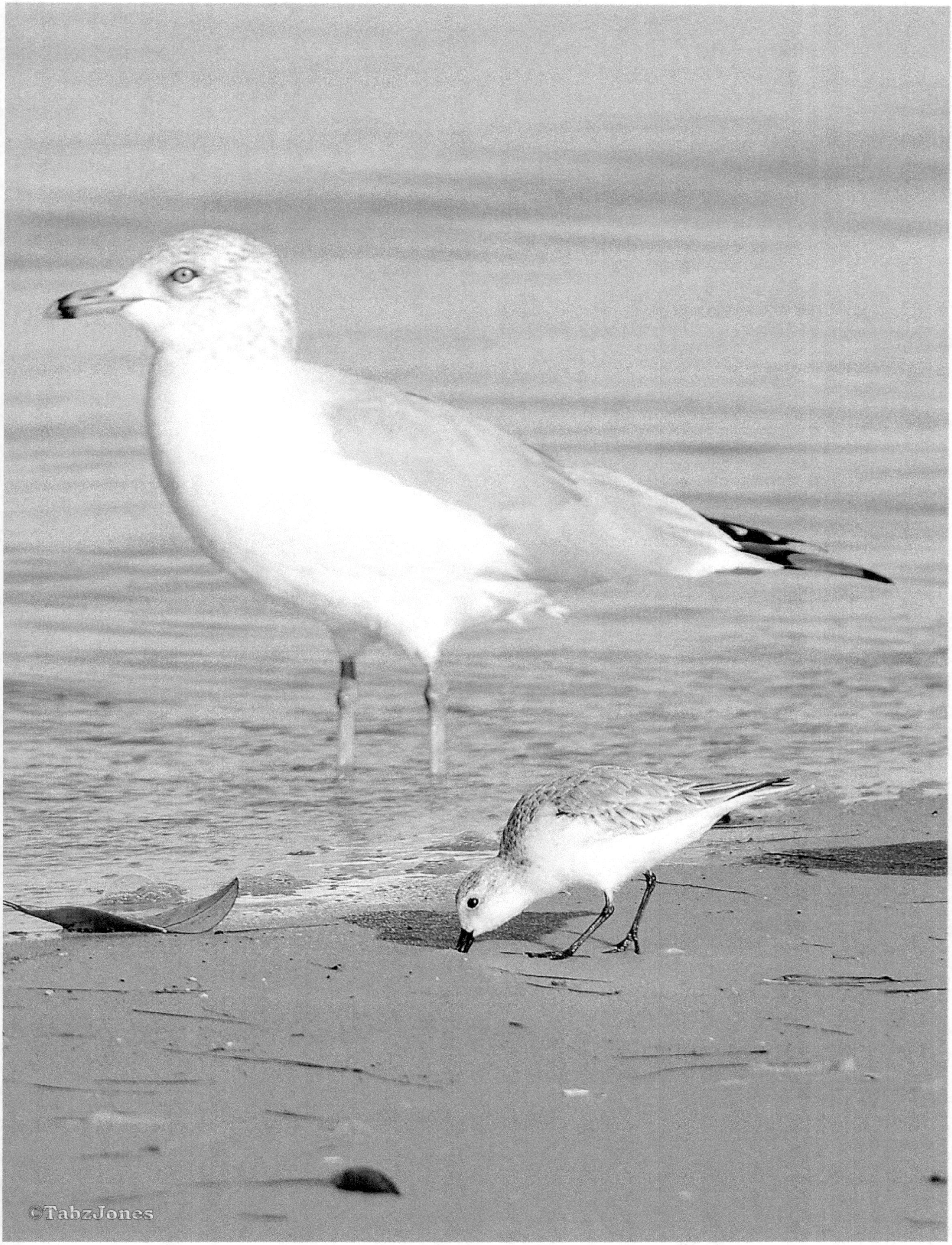
©TabzJones

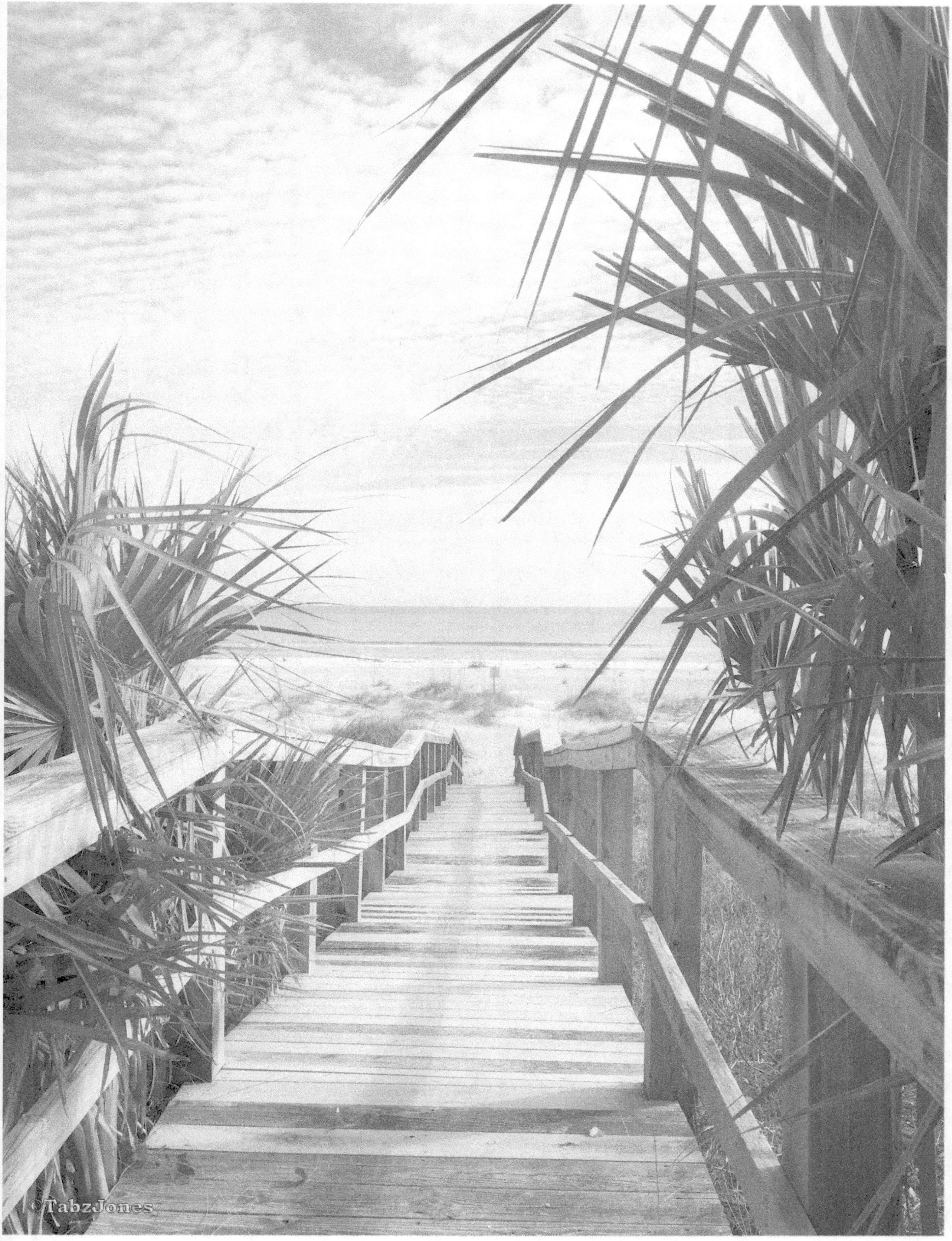
©TabzJones

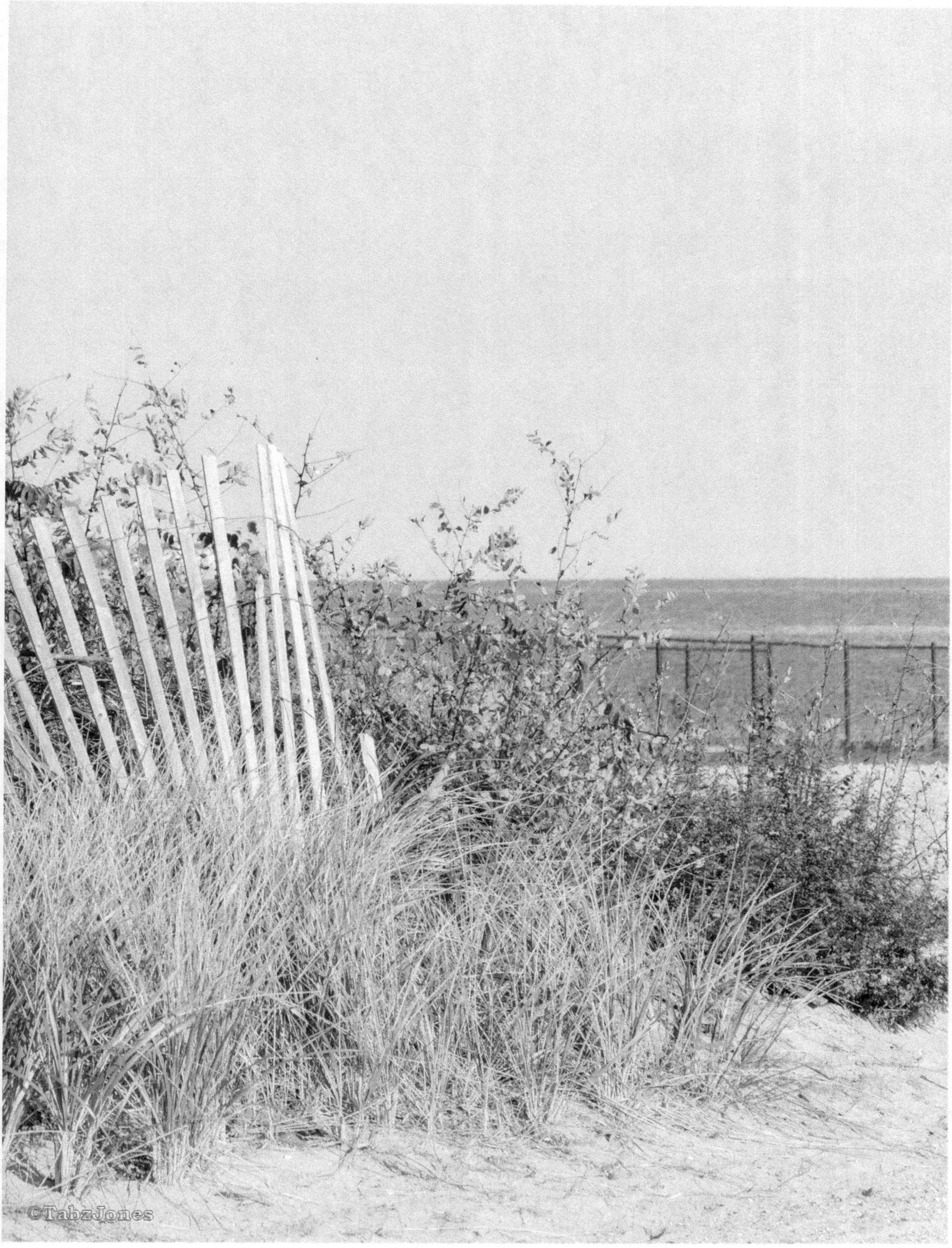
©TabzJones

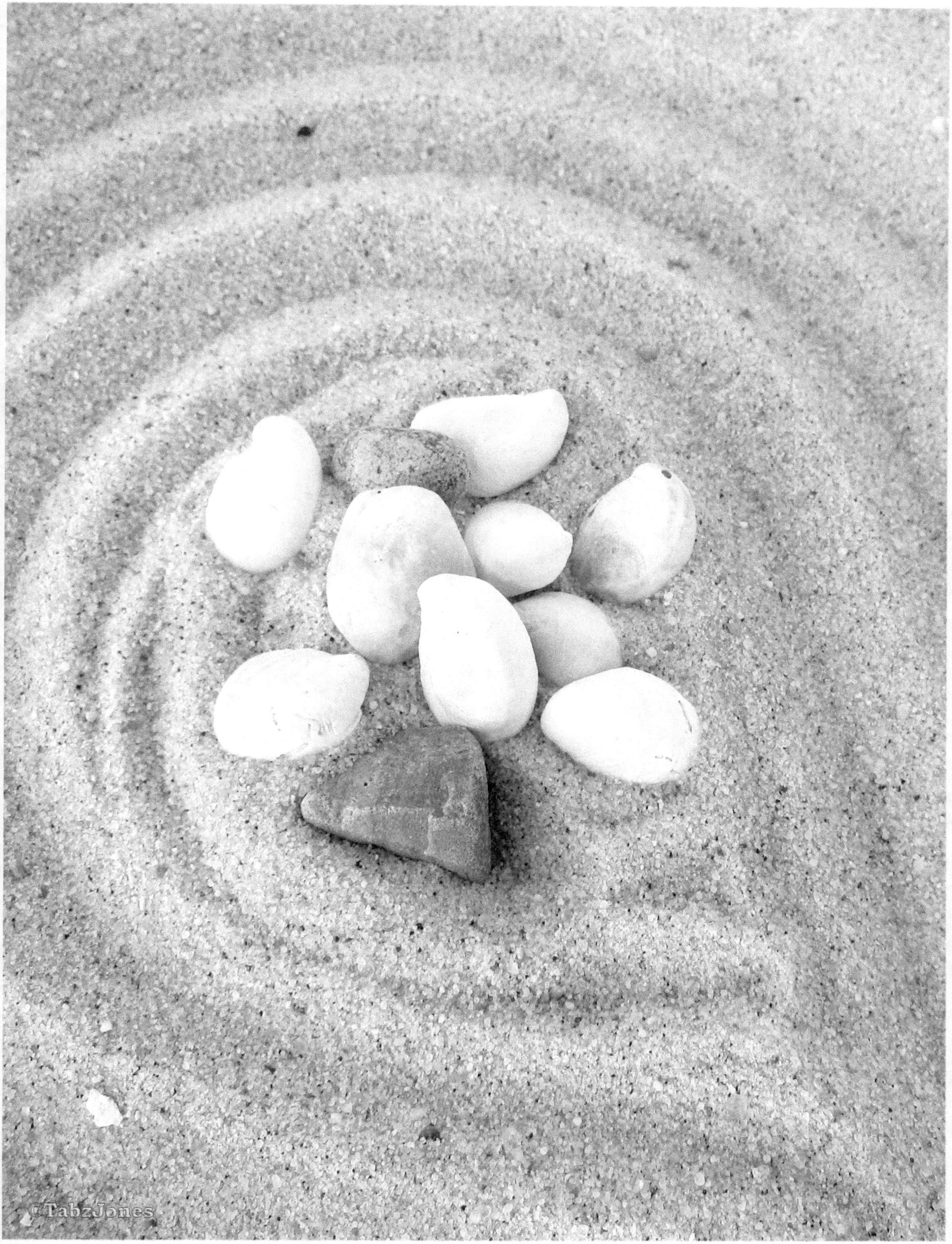

@TabzJones

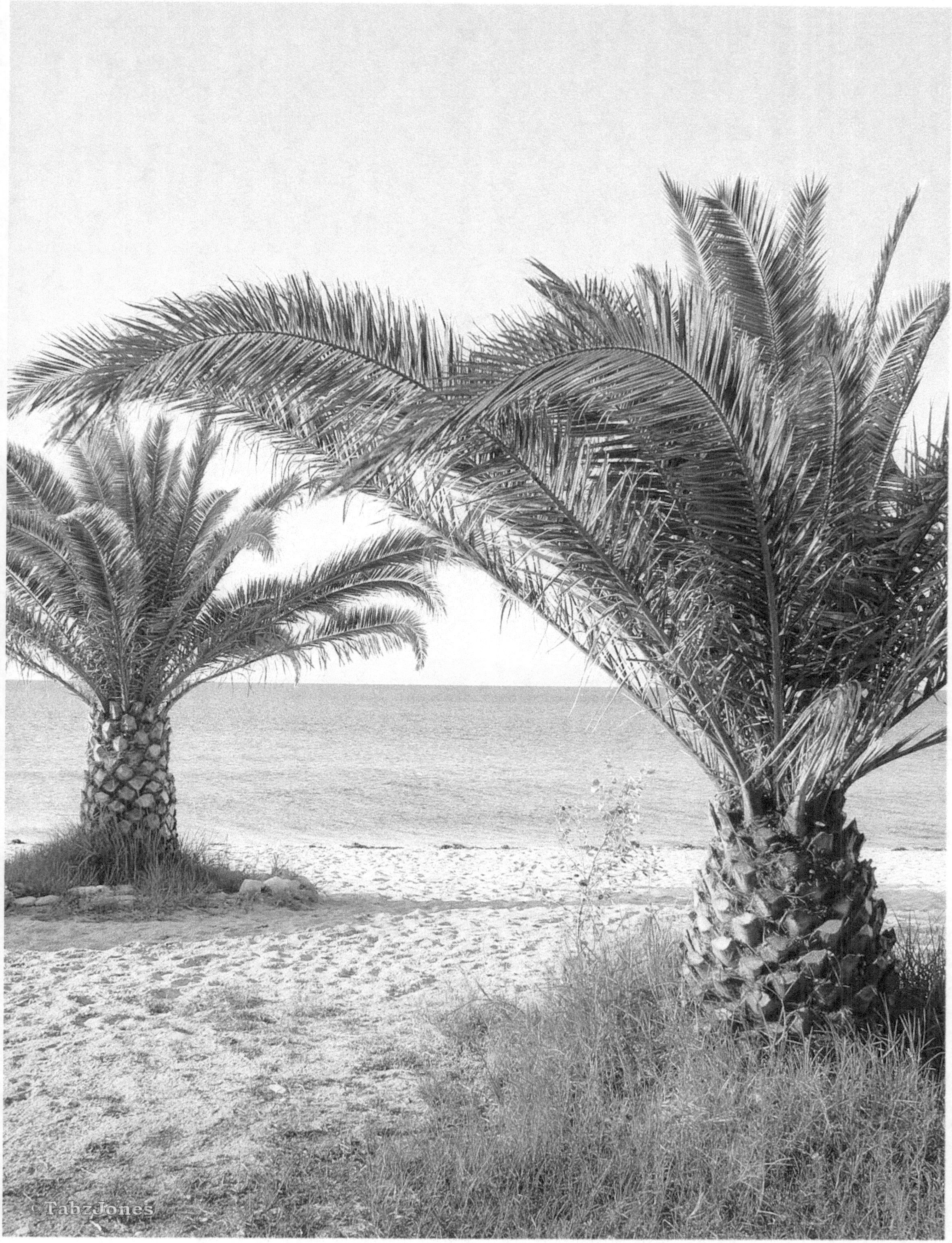
©TabzJones

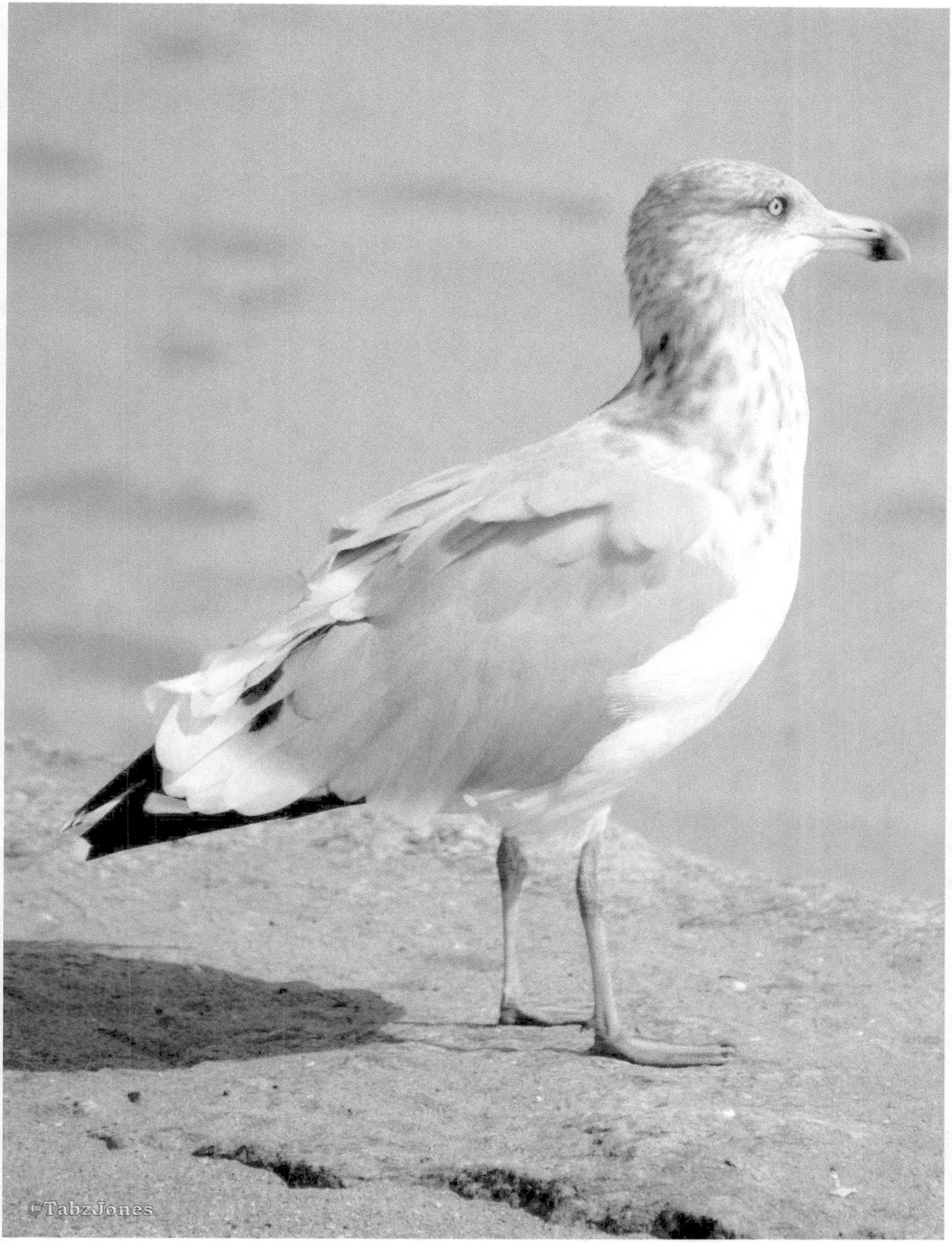
©TabzJones

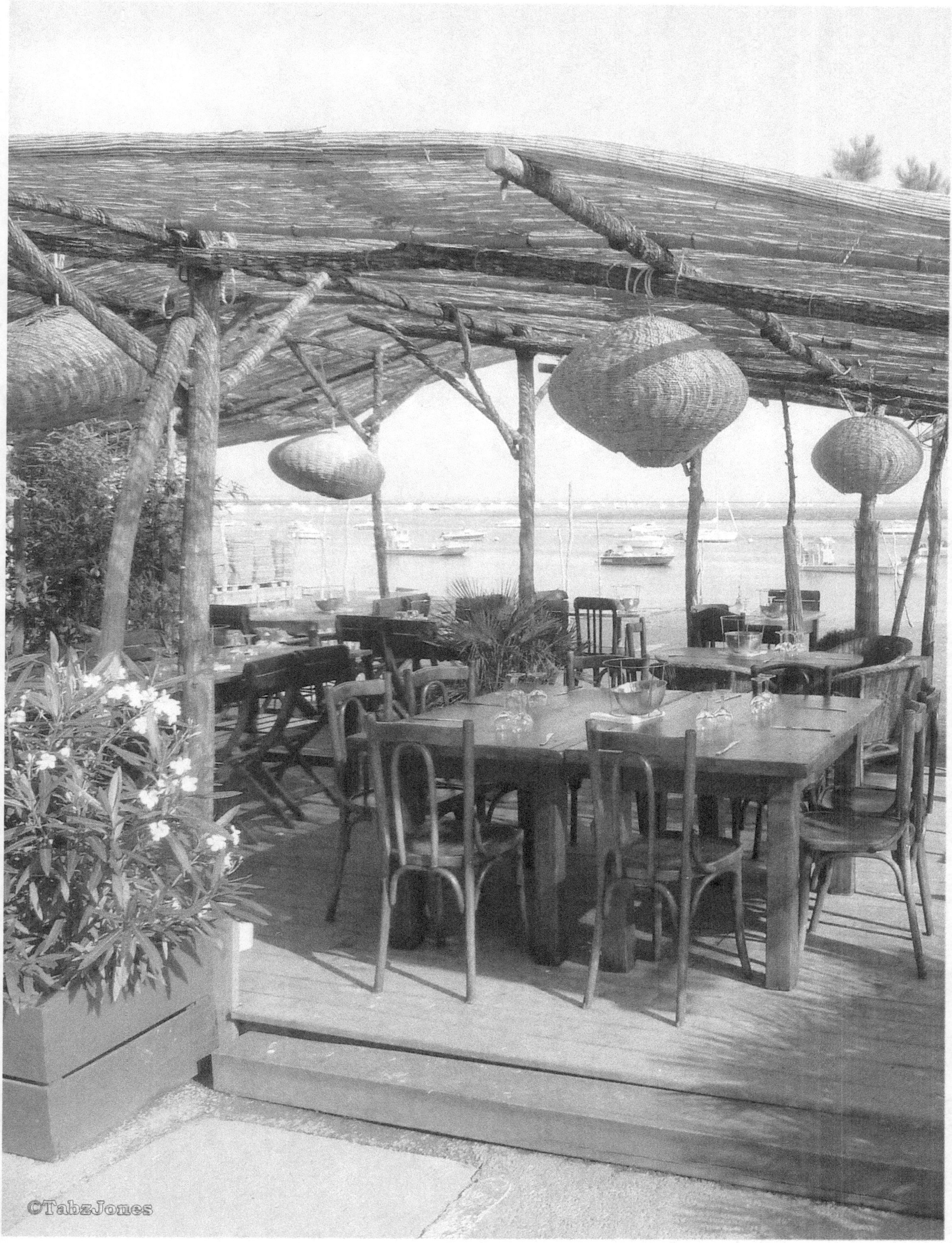
©TabzJones

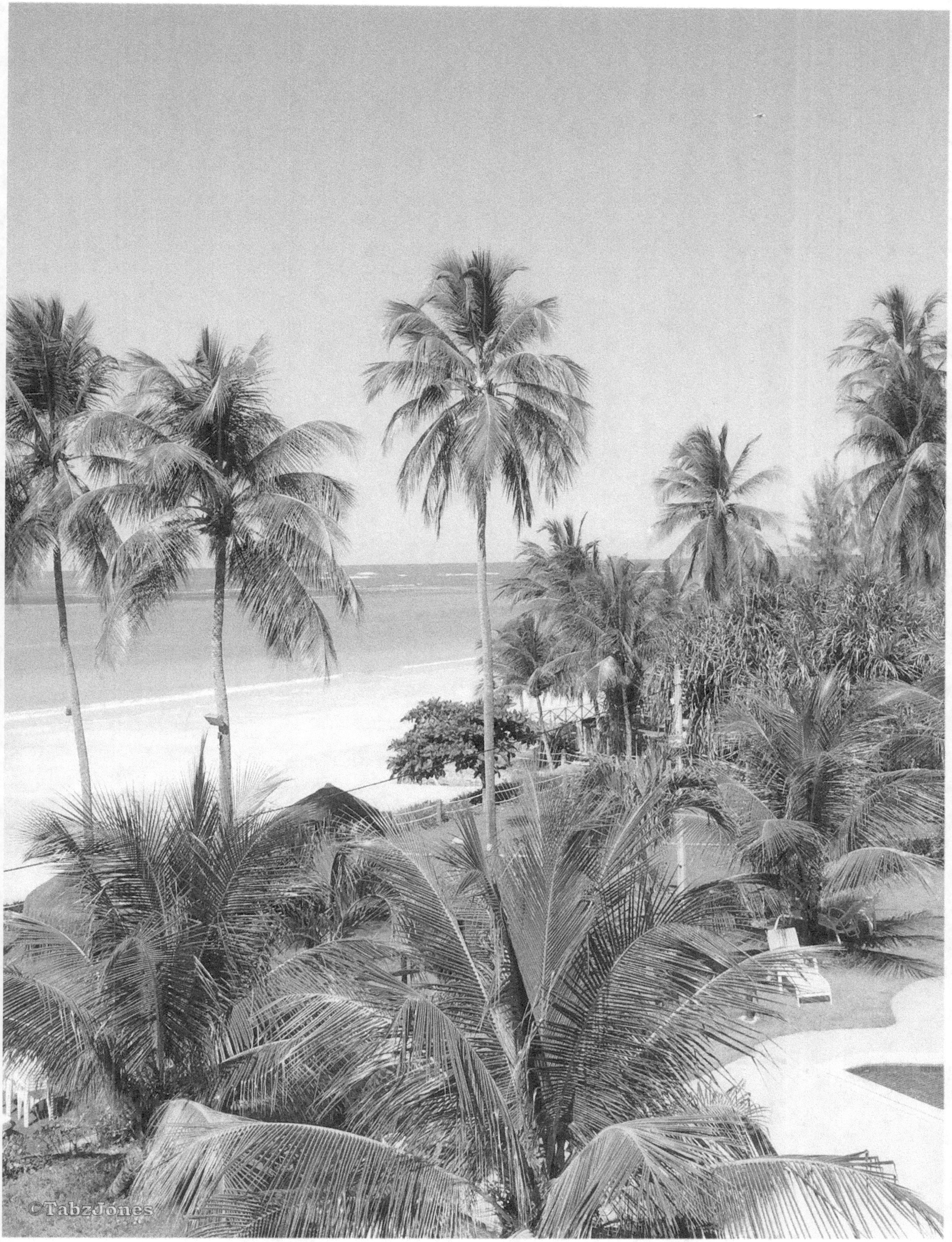
©TabzJones

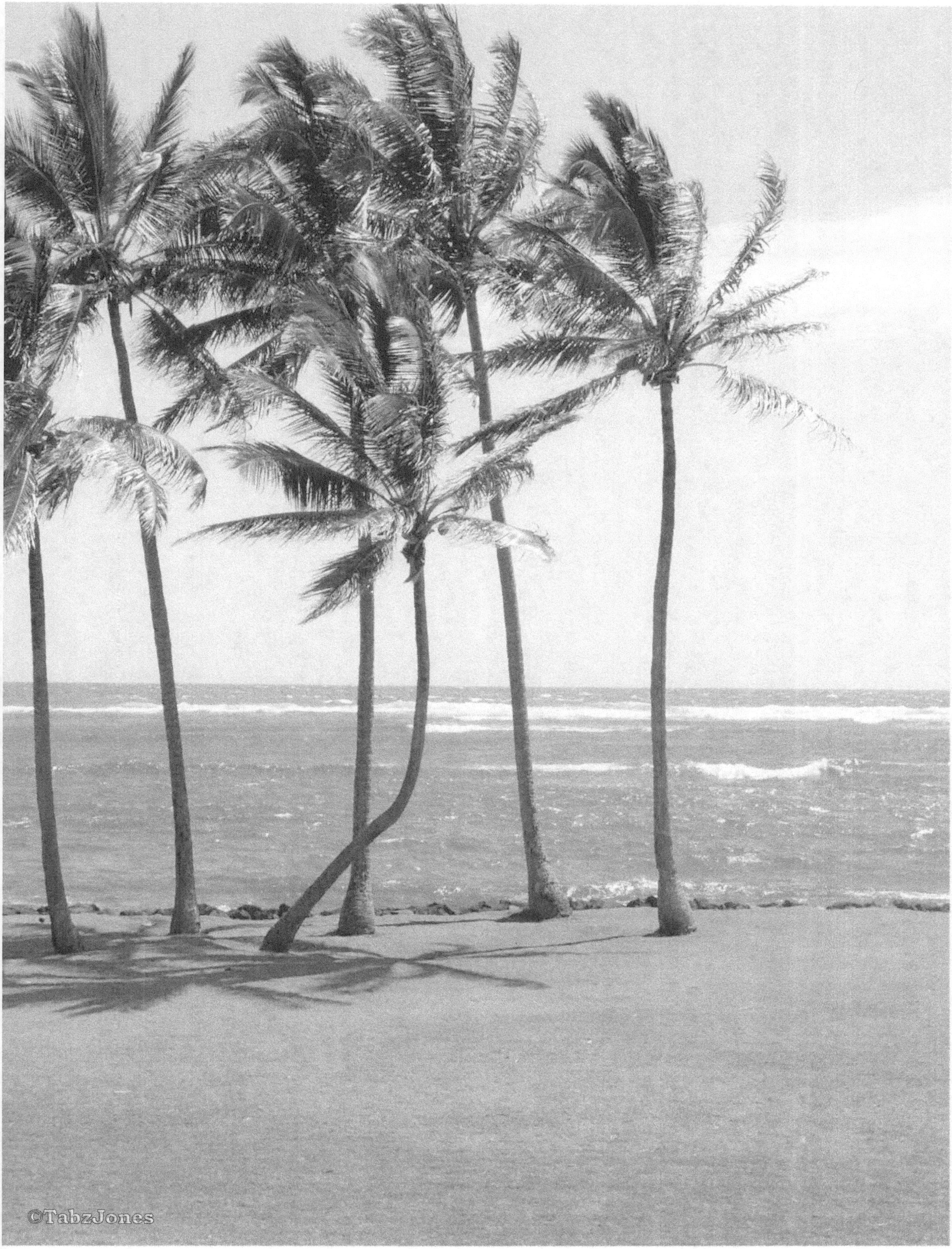
©TabzJones

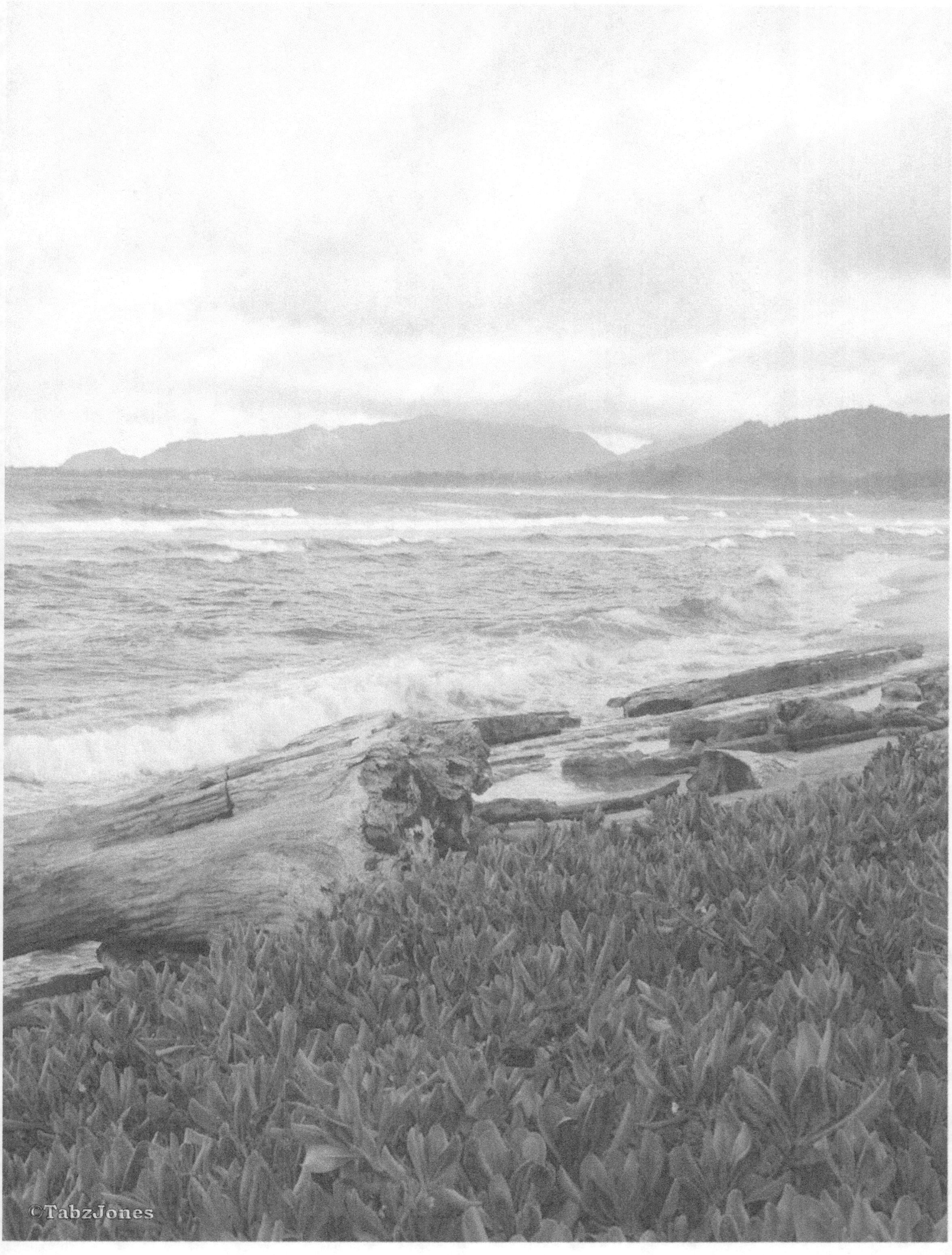
©TabzJones

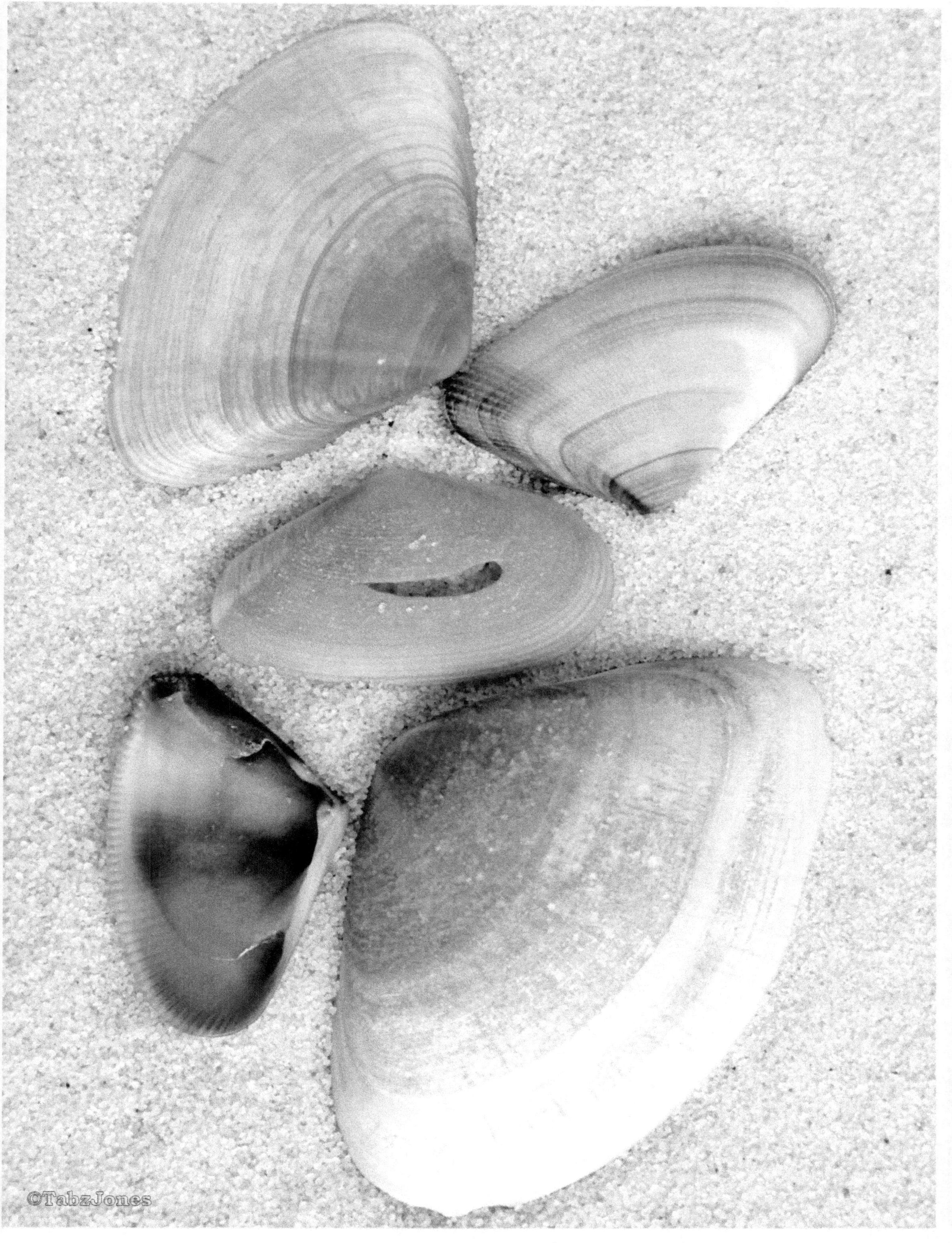
©TabzJones

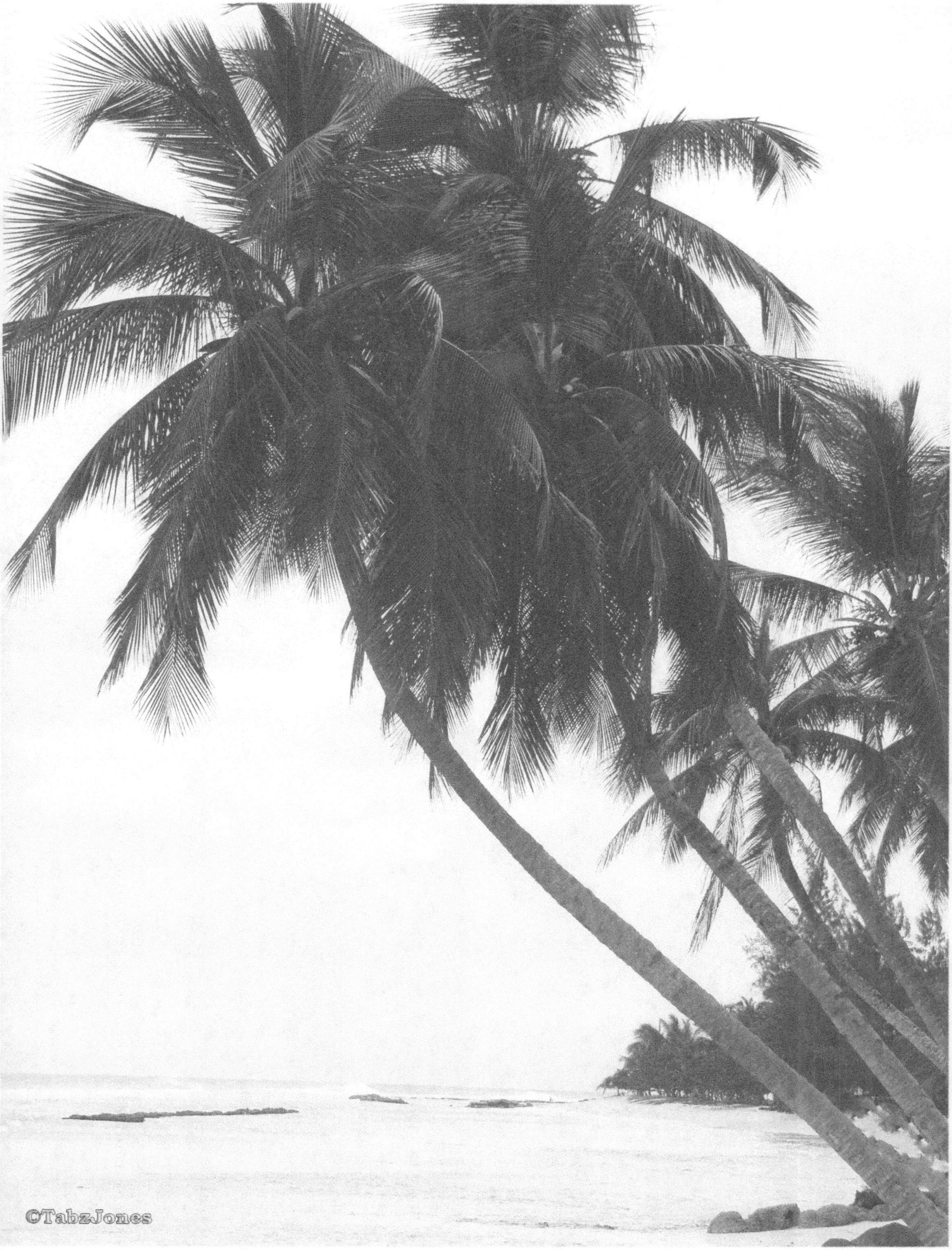
©TabzJones

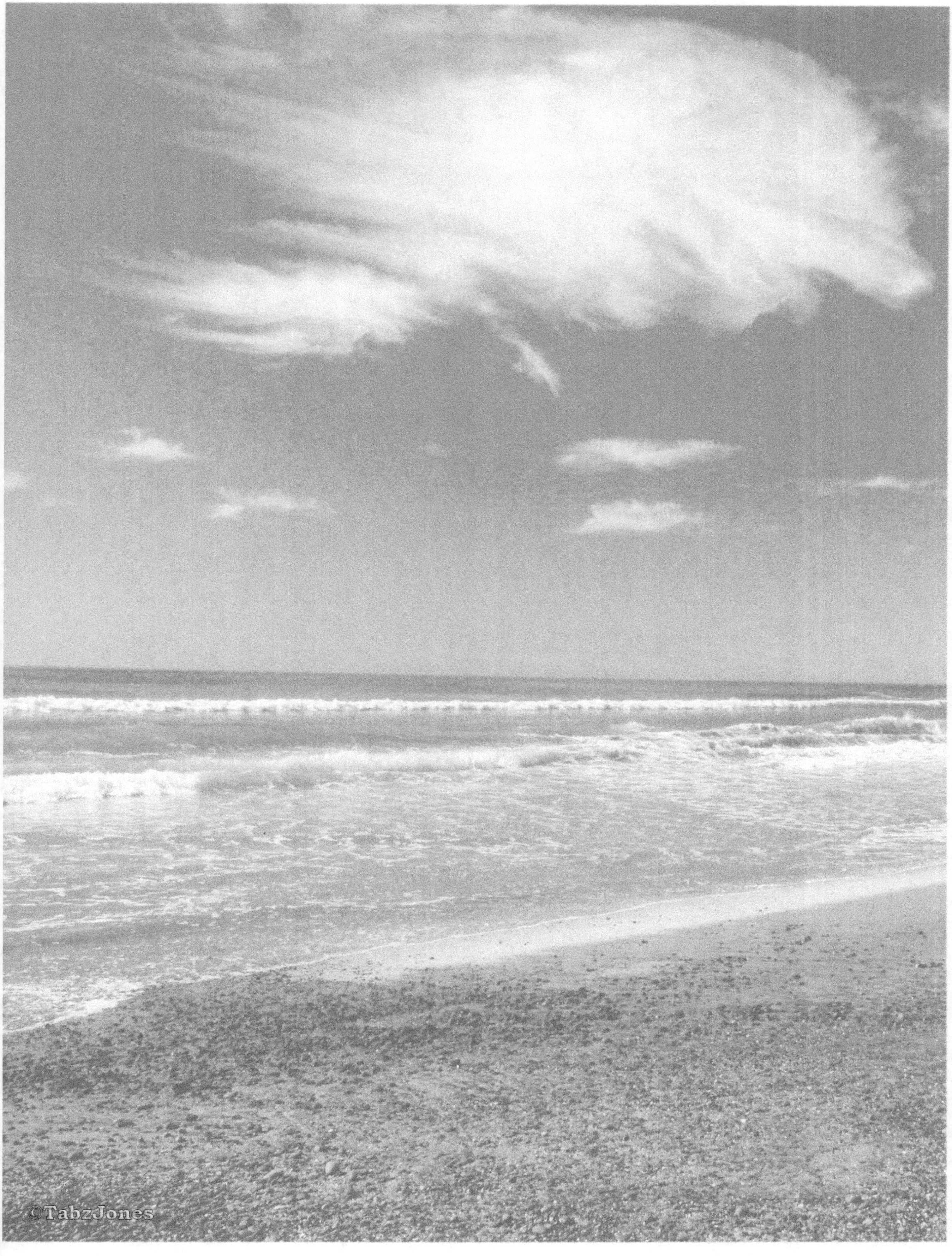
©TabzJones

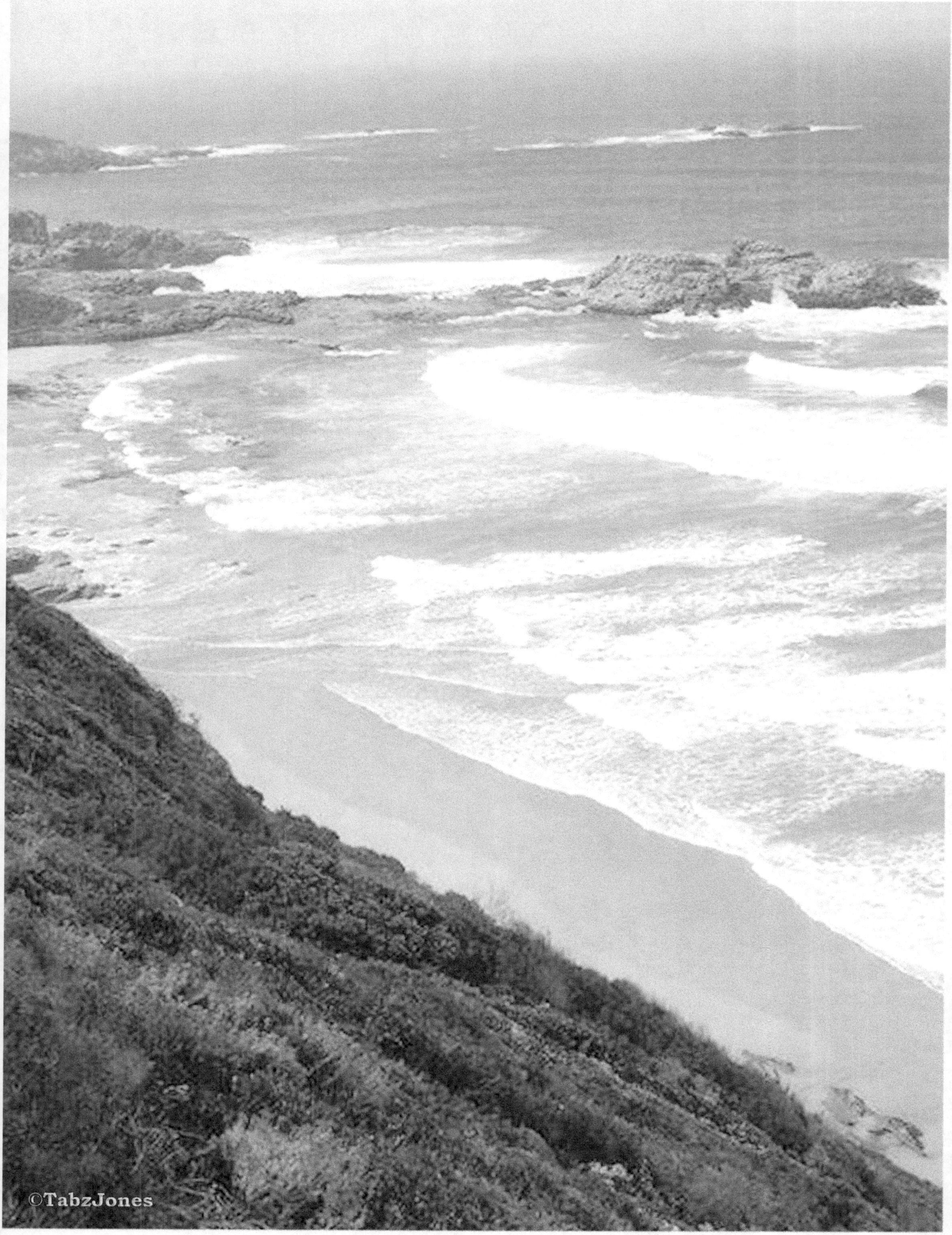
©TabzJones

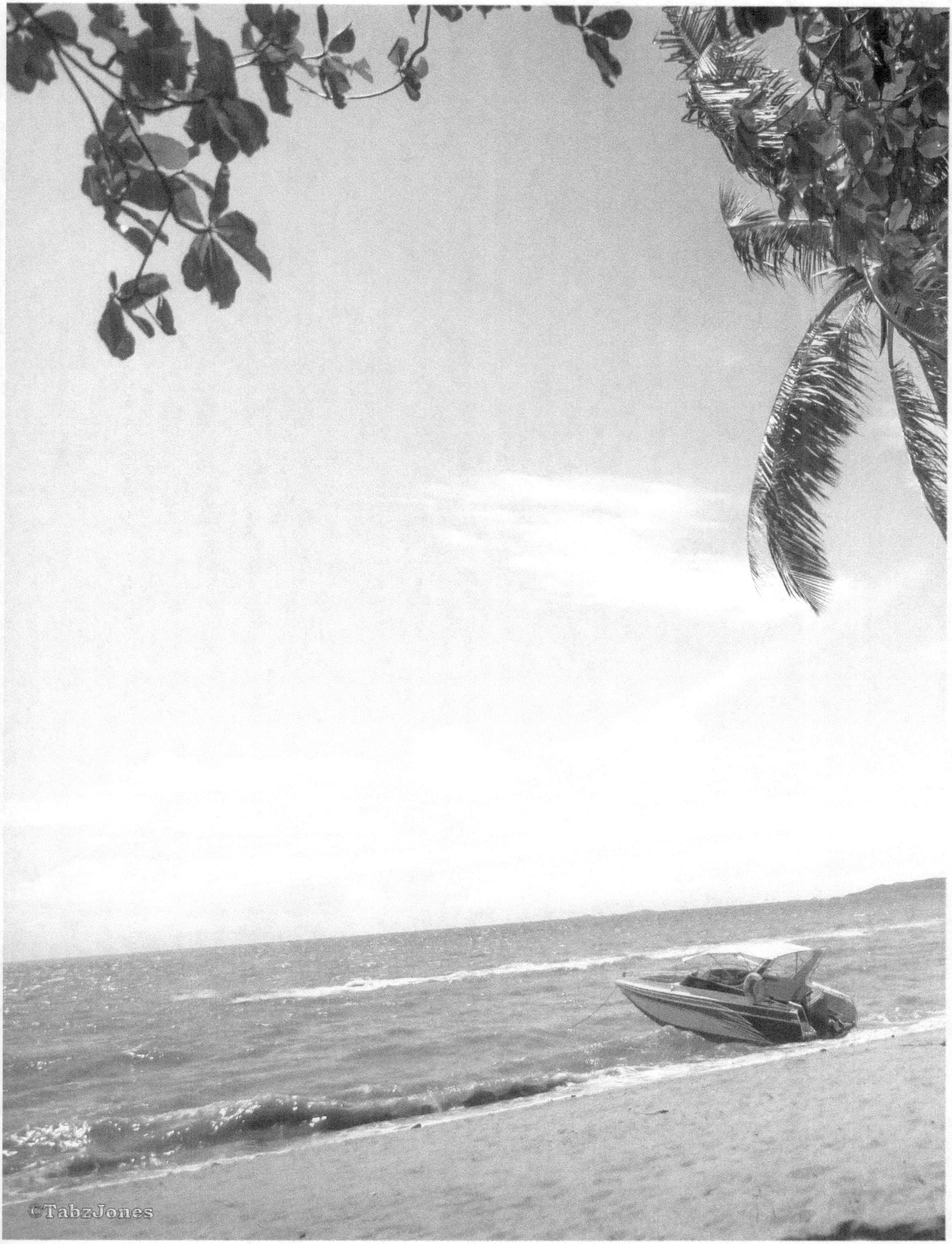
©TabzJones

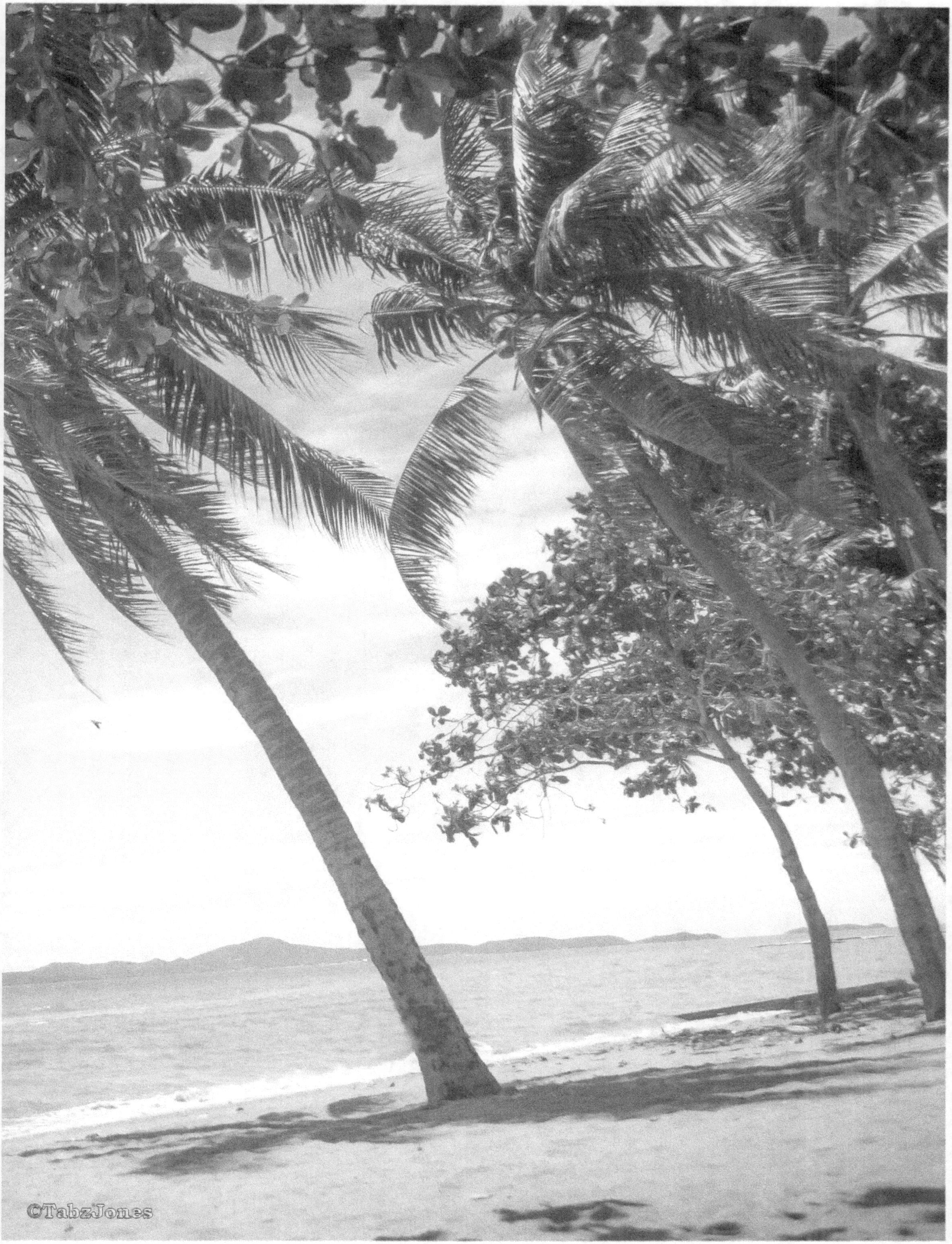
©TabzJones

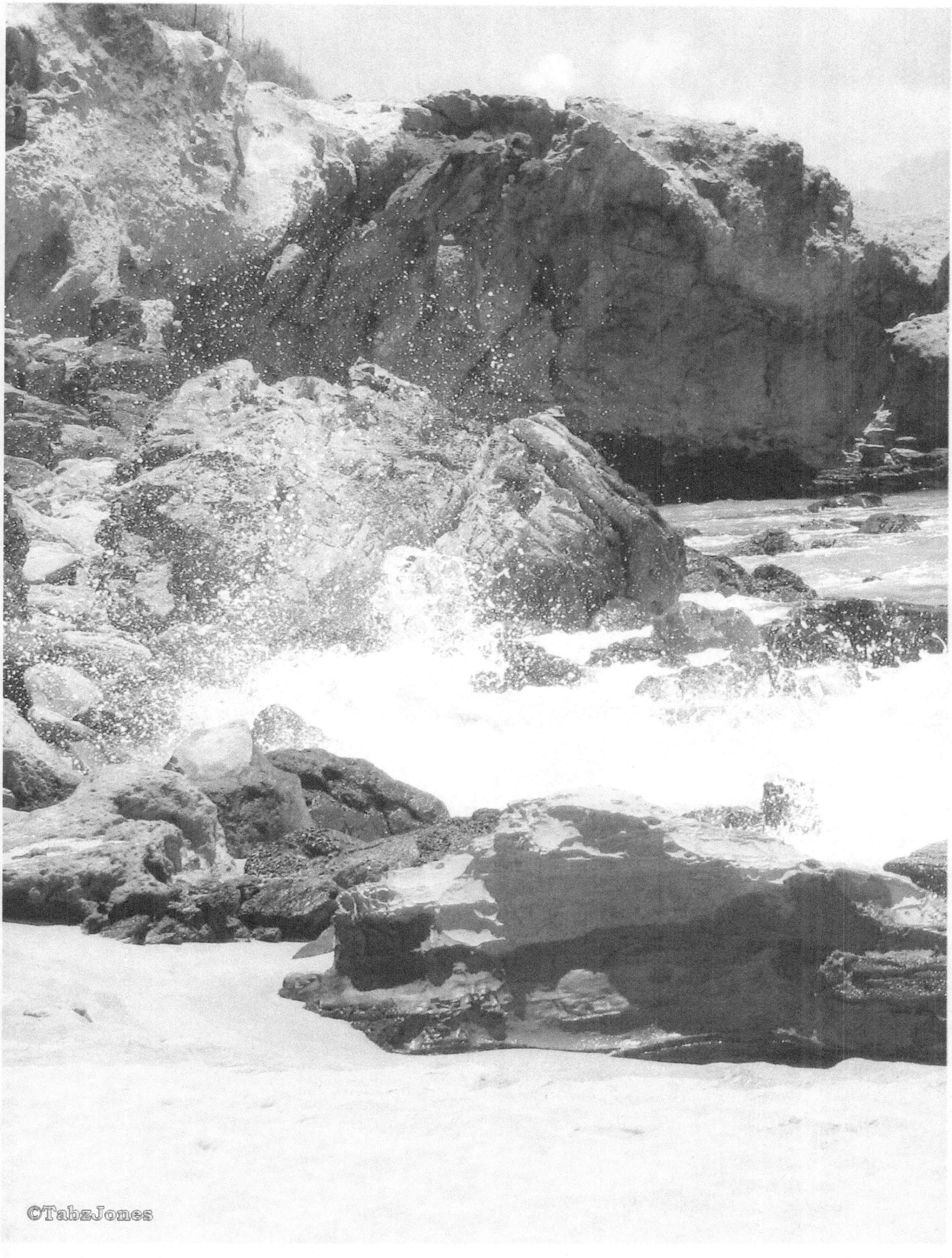
©TabzJones

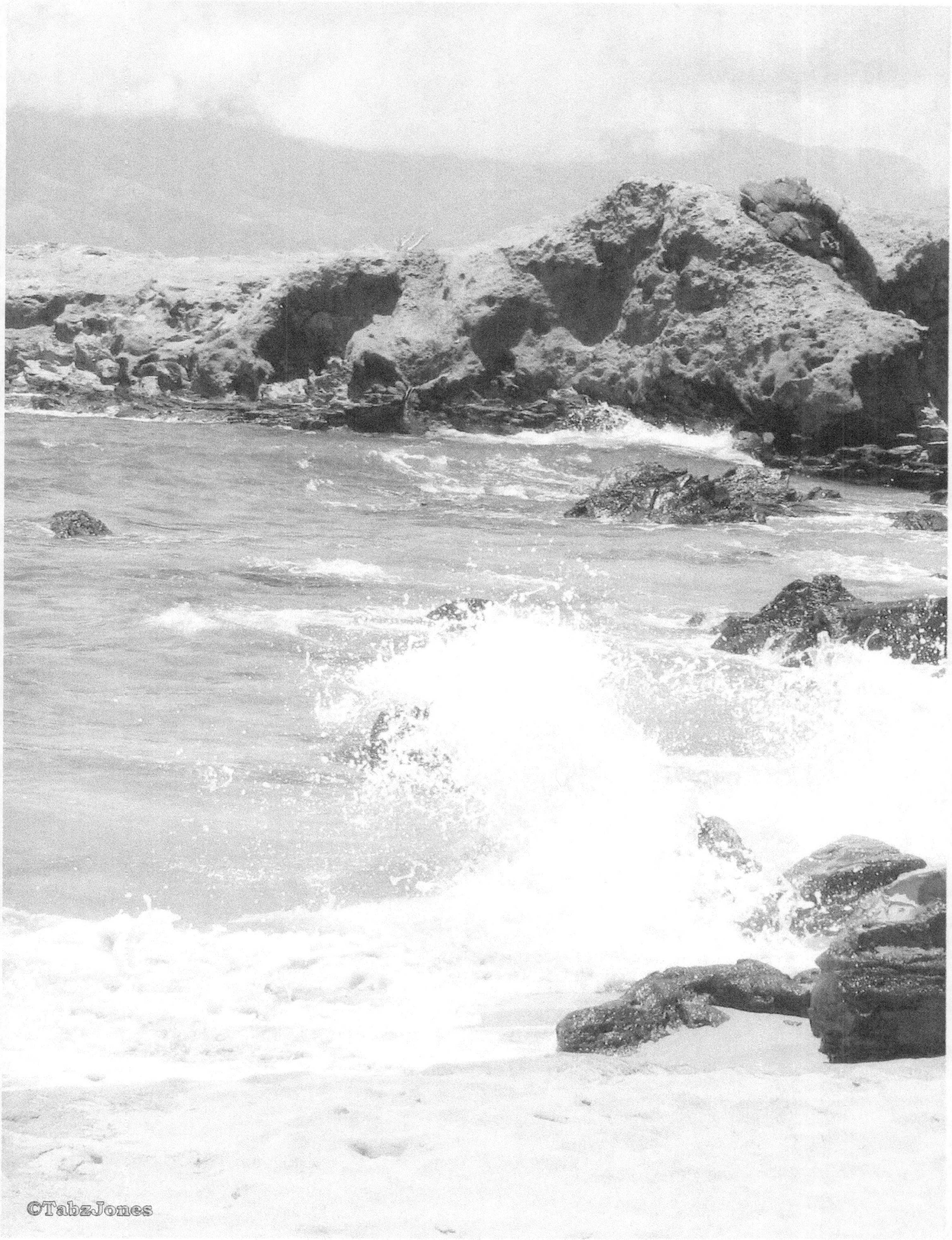
©TabzJones

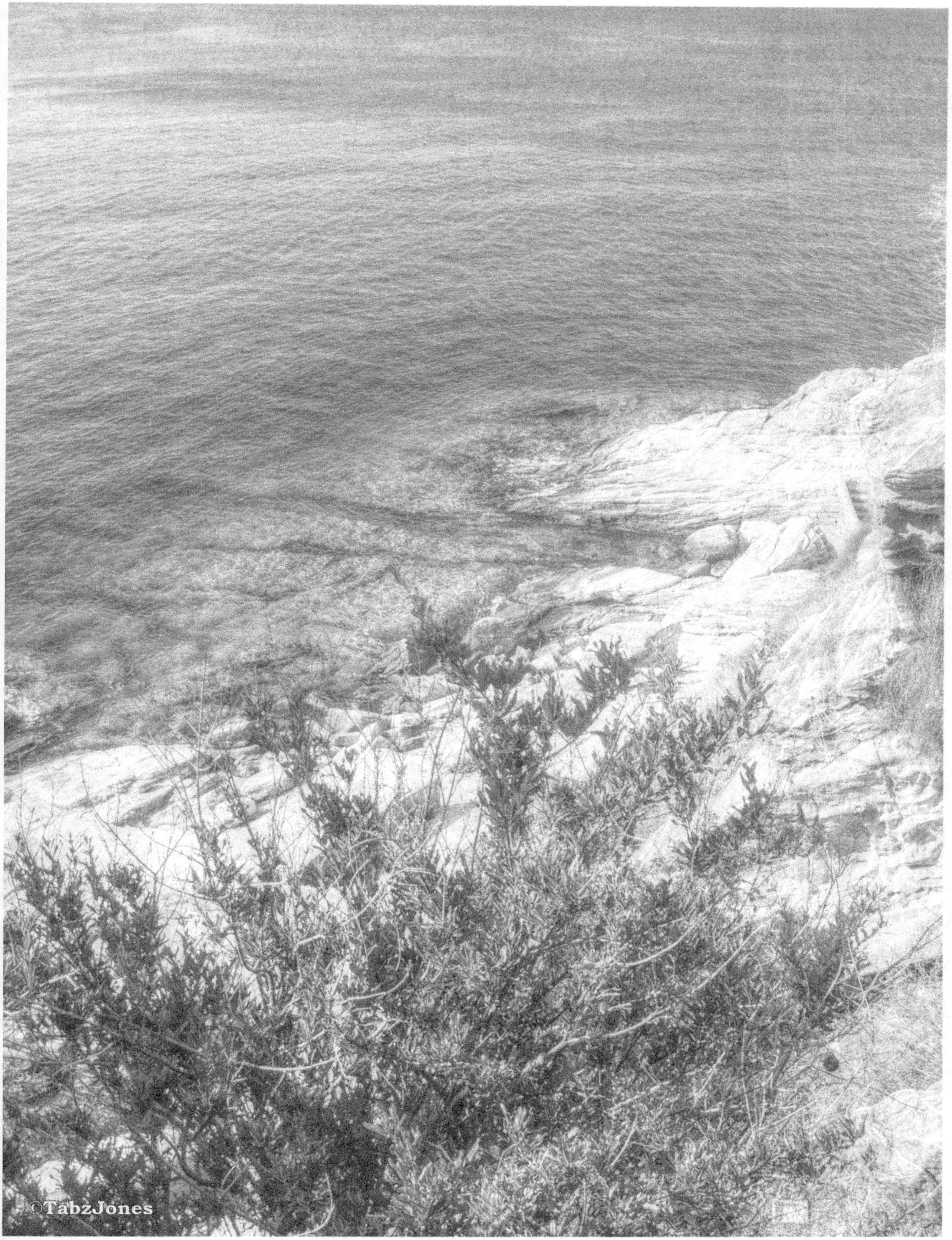
©TabzJones

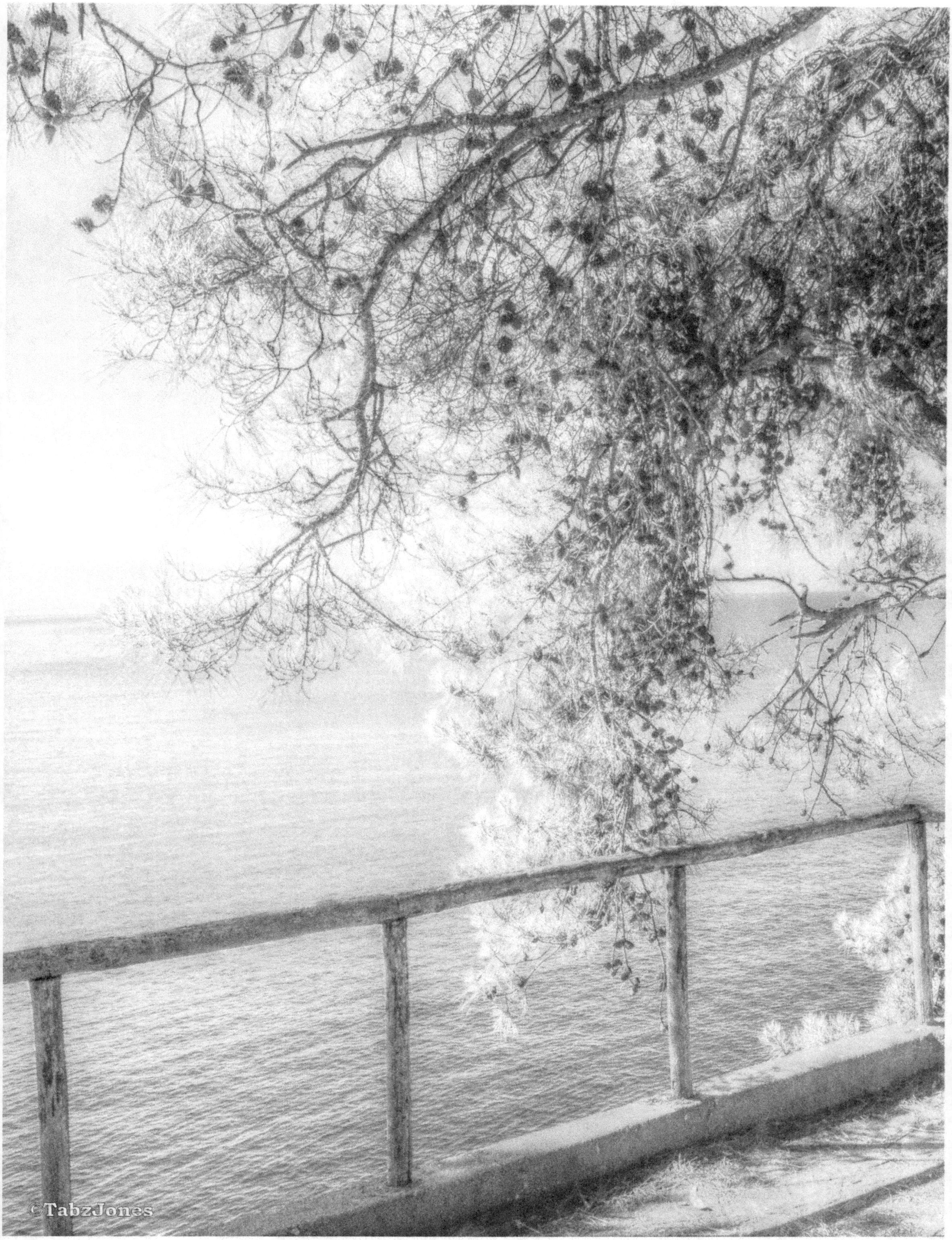
©TabzJones

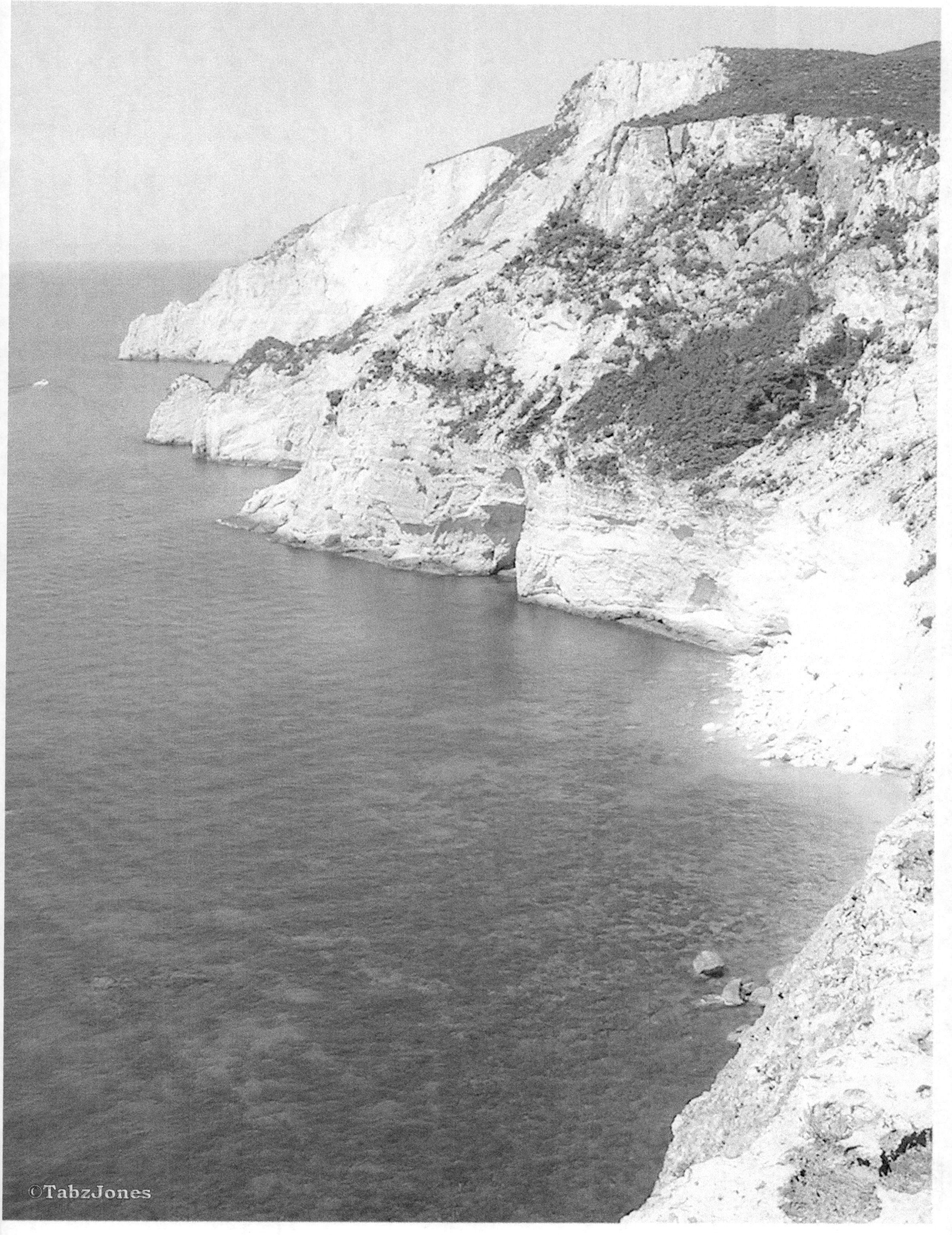
©TabzJones

www.ingramcontent.com/pod-product-compliance
Lightning Source LLC
Chambersburg PA
CBHW080605190526
45169CB00007B/2880
* 9 7 8 1 5 3 0 9 4 1 7 8 0 *